HOW TO INVEST IN REAL ESTATE? A ABSOLUTE GUIDE TO MANAGE YOUR WEALTH IN REIT'S

2

Contents

5

FORWARD

Real estate investment definition

By employing real estate assets as an investment vehicle, real estate investing generates profits via a variety of ways. Simple methods to achieve it include owning real estate, producing cash flow via rental income, and selling the asset for additional money due to appreciation.

Real estate investment, when done well, has the potential to outperform the stock market and create wealth that will last generations. There are four main ways to make money from owning real estate. Among them are dividends from owning real estate investment trust (REIT) shares, rental income, capital gains, supplementary investment income, and so on.

• Property investors use a range of strategies to make money from real estate investments.

• Flipping homes, renting them out, holding REIT shares, auxiliary income, internet real estate platforms, etc. are all examples of real estate investments.

• Real estate may create generational wealth, despite the fact that it is difficult to estimate the genuine average historical return for real estate investors.

• Real estate investment offers several advantages, including passive rental income, property appreciation, investment leverage, and favorable tax treatment.

Why Should I Invest in Properties?

Motives for Real Estate Investing

Real estate investment may add a lot of money to your bank account, but it also has potential risks and requires study. Here are a few of the most significant justifications for real estate investment. (Just keep in mind that neither appreciation nor cash flow is certain. To improve your chances of making a profit, you must do research on homes and communities.)

Regular Cash Flow

Owning a home might boost your monthly income. If you purchase either residential or commercial real estate, you may rent out your space to tenants. You will thereafter receive monthly rent payments in the mail. Just be careful: You'll need to check their payment records if you want to reduce the possibility that your tenants may one day stop paying their rent.

Large Returns

If your real estate's value increases over time, you may be able to sell it for a substantial profit. However, remember that acceptance isn't a given. You must invest in the right sort of real estate to get such big returns.

. Long-Term Stability

Since real estate is a long-term investment, it may be kept for a number of years while you wait for its value to rise. Renting out your house might help you generate a monthly income while you wait for its value to rise.

Diversification

Your financial diversification is increased when you include real estate, which helps shield you from market fluctuations. Let's say that a downturn in the economy is causing some equities to suffer. Your portfolio of investment properties may still be rising in value, shielding you from the losses your other assets are suffering.

Financial Leverage Capacity

You most likely don't have the money to purchase homes outright when investing in real estate. Considering that you want to rent a single-family house, the price may be as high as $200,000. Leverage has a role in this. Real estate leverage refers to the act of buying properties with the assistance of other people's funds. In this scenario, you would borrow money from banks, mortgage companies, or credit unions and gradually pay it back. By doing this, you may increase the amount of real estate you possess without having to pay the whole price to do so.

Deflationary Avoidance

Real estate investments are seen as inflation hedges. Rents and home prices often increase in tandem with rising expenses for goods and services. While a result, investment properties might provide you rising monthly income and capital gains to help you protect your finances while the cost of everything else increases.

Chance to Build Capital

Increasing your cash flow, often known as building capital, is one of the main goals of real estate investing. When you sell a property whose value has improved, your capital will grow. Clearly, the trick is to make the right investments in properties that will appreciate in value.

Control and Contentment

Having an investment property comes with additional non-financial benefits. Being your own boss is beneficial for many investors, which is made possible by owning investment property. Other ways you might improve your community include offering rental housing or luring businesses to commercial locations that will provide much-needed services to nearby areas.

The three main categories of real estate assets are as follows:

1.   Residential: Buildings with one to four apartments. Mom-and-pop investors choose this kind of real estate investment since it is the most regulated and well-liked.

2.   Commercial: This broad classification covers office space, retail, industrial, multifamily (5+ units) apartment complexes, and other sorts of commercial real estate.

3.   Land: Whether it is fully undeveloped, partially developed, or used for farming, land may be a very rewarding investment, but it has its own peculiarities and requires specialized understanding.

Every SMART Investor Should Set Real Estate Goals.

What Are SMART Goals in Real Estate?

Did you know that companies with well-defined objectives are 10 times more successful than those without them? According to a recent research by Harvard Business University, 83 percent of people do not establish objectives, and of those who do, 92 percent fail to fulfill them. First of all, why do so few individuals make goals? Second, why don't more individuals succeed in achieving those objectives? The answer is straightforward: most individuals don't create sensible objectives.

- Specific

- Measurable

- Attainable

- Relevant

- Time-bound

You may utilize the acronym S.M.A.R.T. to direct the goal-setting process for your real estate firm.

- Business Objectives: An organization may have objectives ranging from lead creation to team expansion. For instance, one corporate objective may be to get 10% more social media followers over the course of the next six months. Both paid web advertising and word-of-mouth marketing might be used for this. Three wholesale agreements might be completed in a year as a corporate objective for investment deals. Your company will determine exactly where you should start.

•	Setting personal objectives is a terrific approach to make sure that your growth coincides with that of your investment company. Personal goals often include things like reading a book every month for a year or listening to one investment podcast per week. Personal objectives may assist you in developing new connections, increasing your daily tasks, and increasing your skill set.

•	Family objectives: It's crucial to set aside time for family or friends while investors concentrate on SMART objectives for their professional and personal development. Setting a weekly call-free day to spend more time with your loved ones is a great example of a family goal. Similar to this, many investors may decide to take time off for the holidays or to organize a family trip. Keep in mind that while you develop a prosperous real estate company, these objectives may be crucial for fostering equilibrium.

How can you make wise real estate investments?

- Business Techniques
- Fix-and-Flip. Finding homes that require work, making the necessary repairs, and then reselling them for top dollar

to make a profit is known as the "fix-and-flip" method.

- Wholesaling, house hacking, live-in-then-rent, live-in-flip, BRRRR investing, short-term buy and hold rentals, long-term buy and hold rentals, and live-in-then-rent all fall under this category.

Which real estate tactic is the most profitable?

Appreciation

Real estate appreciation—an rise in the property's value that is recognized when you sell—is the most typical technique to generate money in the industry. The main factors influencing the value of residential and commercial real estate are location, development, and upgrades.

How can risk tolerance be evaluated?

Investors are often questioned in order to determine their risk tolerance. Assessing their time horizon, available assets, and need for income, as well as their comfort level with enduring market volatility and remaining invested during a market collapse, might be part of this.

What does real estate risk tolerance mean?

The level or kind of risk that an investor can bear or is ready to accept. Real estate purchases, for instance, may be quite lucrative. The property may be improved by an investor, who can then resell it for a lot more money.

How can risk in real estate be analyzed?

The hazards involved vary depending on your project's specifics and the real estate asset in question. Real estate risk analysis may be done using a variety of techniques, such as break-even analysis, quantitative analysis, and financial index analysis, among others.

How well do you comprehend the real estate market?

- Real Estate Market Analysis: 6 Steps in Detail
- Investigate the facilities and quality of the community.

- Obtain local property value estimations.
- For your real estate market study, choose comparables.
- Determine the average listing price for similar properties.
- Adjust your comparables to fine-tune your market analysis.

What aspect of real estate is most crucial?

The Most Crucial Considerations in Real Estate Investing

The maxim "location, location, location" is still true and is still the most crucial element in real estate investment success.

How can one do local real estate market research?

How to Conduct an Analysis of the Real Estate Market

- Step 1: Pick a neighborhood or particular location.
- Step 2: Investigate Your Rivals.
- Step 3: Research the Neighborhoods You Want.
- Step 4: Inspect the physical aspects of the area or the property.
- Step 5: Assess the performance of the area.

What are the conditions of the local real estate market?

In a nutshell, when there are more houses for sale than there are potential purchasers, property prices fall. When there are fewer available properties than there are prospective buyers, house prices will increase. When there are almost as many homes up for sale as there are buyers, the market is said to be balanced.

How should a neighborhood market be evaluated?

A thorough marketing study should answer the following questions:

Who are my potential customers?

What buying patterns do my customers have?

What is the size of my target market?

What range of prices will customers accept for my offering?

Who are my main competitors?

What are the benefits and drawbacks of my competitors?

Options for Financing a Real Estate Investment

Cash will be used to finance your home.

The first choice is to pay the whole cost of the property up front in cash. Naturally, in order to achieve this, you must have the required materials on hand. Benefits: Since the seller's worries regarding financing are removed when you pay in full up front, your chances of successfully purchasing a home rise. In exchange for the simplicity that cash offers, purchasing with cash enables you to buy residences at significant discounts. Customers who pay in cash also avoid the hefty interest fees associated with conventional, hard-money, or private loans.

Cons: In this situation, risk against reward is important. Cash payments are more secure and prudent, but they have a limit on how much you may make. Think about it like this: If you spend $250,000 in cash and subsequently rent the property for $2,000 per month, you will get $24,000 in gross revenue year, or a 9.6% gross return on investment. As an alternative, your monthly principle and interest payment would be $977 if you placed $50,000 down and took out a 30-year loan at 5%.

You may use a private individual lender to finance your property.

Lenders that do business independently of financial institutions are known as private individuals. Lending money to people who raise the value of their investment properties is often how they earn a profit.

Advantages: Compared to established institutions, private lenders are often far more flexible in who they will lend money to and how fast they may do so. You may gain in a variety of ways if they consider you to be a wise investment. This could be excellent if you don't meet the standard mortgage profile (for example, if your credit is poor).

Hard-money loans may be used to finance your property.

Some borrowers deal with private lenders in this way. It is known as a "hard loan" since it is backed by a tangible asset, in this instance, real estate. This loan is a kind of bridge loan, a brief-term arrangement that provides money until the home can be sold or a more reliable source of finance can be found.

Obtain standard bank financing for your home.

The most typical kind of funding is this. A financial institution in this instance gives money to the borrower based on their credit history and potential to repay the loan.

Benefits: While interest rates on loans for investment properties are greater than those for mortgages for main residences, utilizing this option often results in lower interest rates than using a private lender. Additionally, as previously said, depending on how much cash you have available for a down payment, financing via a bank may optimize your potential return.

Cons: Risk is one of the possible issues. Having a mortgage payment during a rental property vacancy might significantly reduce your revenues. Borrowers may only have a certain number of traditional mortgages open at once, and banks have considerably tougher lending criteria and a much lengthier approval procedure than private lenders.

Indications That You Should Purchase an Investment Property

You're in good financial standing

In particular, if you want to rent the property out to renters, investment properties demand a far greater degree of financial stability than personal residences. For investment homes, the majority of mortgage lenders demand borrowers to put down at least 15% of the purchase price, however this is often not necessary when purchasing your first house. Investment property owners in several states also need to get their dwellings approved by inspectors before renting out their properties, in addition to making a larger down payment.

Make sure your budget includes enough money to pay for both the initial expenditures of buying a property (such as your down payment, inspection fees, and closing charges) and ongoing upkeep and repairs. You must make necessary repairs as a landlord or owner of a rental property quickly, which may require costly emergency plumbing and HVAC repairs. In several places, renters have the right to withhold rent payments if you don't promptly remedy any malfunctioning house utilities.

Return on Investment, or ROI for short, exists.

Real estate investors often see positive cash flow from their investments in today's market, but the best ones calculate their expected return on investment (ROI) rates in advance of making a purchase. To calculate your ROI on potential real estate investments, follow these steps.

Determine your annual rental income. Search for similar homes that are up for rent. Multiply the typical monthly rent for the sort of house you're interested in by 12 to get the cost for a year.

Find out what your net operating profit is. After calculating your potential annual rental income, determine your net operating income. Your net operational income is the annual rental estimate minus your operating expenses. All of your operating expenses are included in your yearly property maintenance charges. Resident's association dues, insurance, and property taxes are a few expenses. Exclude the mortgage or interest when determining your net operating expenditures. Subtract your operational expenses from the anticipated annual rent to get your net operating income.

Analyze your ROI. Subtract your net operating income from the total of your mortgage to get your overall return on investment (ROI).

AN ANALYSIS OF THE REAL ESTATE MARKET IN TWO PRIMARY STEPS

Initial Screening at Step 1

In order to concentrate your attention on the most promising areas, the first screen in a real estate market study aims to swiftly exclude markets that aren't a suitable match. Once you've finished a few, this phase may be completed in as little as 10 minutes. I narrowed my first screening down to three "deal breakers" for this exercise.

Data resources

A preformed the accounting records itemizing rentals and net cash flow after expenditures should be provided by the person selling you the property. You may use Zillow.com to research housing costs and rents in the area you're thinking of purchasing in order to verify the preformed' accuracy. Verify the accuracy of the seller's numbers.

Effective Property Management

I generally advise investors to find at least two reputable property managers in every given market since bad property management is the most frequent cause of real estate investments failing. In this manner, you'll know what to fall back on if the first one doesn't work out for whatever reason.

Rather than a mom-and-pop business operating out of a person's home, the property management firm needs to be a legitimate business. A "deep bench" of managers, leasing agents, handymen, etc. should be present to ensure that service won't be disrupted by absences or staff turnover.

Requiring two top-notch property management firms may effectively cut out smaller metro areas. Finding one reputable property management business is challenging enough, much alone two, in a metro area with a population of under 100,000.

Data resources

You should investigate the property management business that is suggested by your landlord to see whether they will work for you. You can: To locate a second (backup) property manager:

Look at the reviews by searching "residential property management" and "city name" on Yelp.com. Focus on landlord ratings instead of the reviews left by irate renters. Visit Meetup.com and look for local real estate investment groups where the property is located. Send a referral request to the Meet up Group's organizer through email.

What does "due diligence" entail in the context of real estate?

Simply said, doing due diligence entails gathering information regarding the property's physical, financial, and geographic conditions. The phrase "doing your homework" before making an offer and after your contract is approved is an excellent way to describe due diligence.

What is the purpose of due diligence for a seller?

By performing their own research before the buyer does, a seller is more inclined to identify what needs to be fixed, corrected, or addressed at their discretion, and with enough time to handle those concerns from their perspective most effectively. In other words, the seller can decide and control the cards they've been dealt.

What tax effects do real estate investments have?

Depreciation is a tax-deductible cost for real estate investors who own rental properties that generate revenue. As a result, you'll likely have a lesser tax burden and less taxable income.

How can I keep from having to pay taxes on my rental property?

By employing tax harvesting or a 1031 delayed exchange, you may avoid paying this tax. As an alternative, you might invest via a retirement account or turn your rental home into your permanent abode. To prevent losing money after making an investment in real estate, don't forget to get your property insured with steadily.

What qualifies as investment property in the eyes of the IRS?
In general, real estate is seen as an investment if it is purchased with the intention of making a profit rather than for personal habitation by you and your family.

It's crucial that you choose the best exit strategy for you in real estate investment since there are several options to take into account.

Your choice is influenced by a number of variables, including:

- Your capacity as a shareholder
- Your coverage of debt service
- Your targets for short-term investments
- Your long-term financial objectives
- Your capacity for risk as an investment.

Define your objectives, educate yourself, choose an investment strategy, make a financial plan, get financing, evaluate properties, understand asset allocation, and pick property management as your first steps in building a real estate portfolio.

Building a solid team, searching for greater value, expanding into new areas, streamlining property administration, and taking into account partnerships and syndications are some tips for growing your real estate portfolio.

How to Begin Your Real Estate Portfolio

The goal of a real estate portfolio is to use a variety of real estate assets together to accomplish a financial goal. Real estate investors should fully comprehend all facets of real estate investing before starting a real estate portfolio, while doing so may be advantageous.

Follow these steps to start creating your real estate portfolio:

Organize your goals.

Setting goals is the first step in launching any successful business. Your personal goals, financial goals, and investment goals are all significant and will influence the path of action. You may establish a plan for accomplishing your goals and make educated financial decisions by setting clear targets. This plan will be essential for guiding the expansion of your real estate holdings.

Choose a spending strategy.

You may start considering what sort of real estate investment strategy to use after you have a firm grasp of the housing market.

Whether you choose to invest in residential, commercial, or a mix of the three kinds of properties is up to you. Consider if you want to focus on making investments in rental property to earn income or look for fix-and-flip opportunities. These decisions will influence the rest of your portfolio-building journey.

Considering homes

You should start looking at homes after you have researched your financing options and found a solution. You should start by doing a thorough market research to identify neighborhoods and houses that match your goals. You may then evaluate each property and do your due diligence on it after doing this. The key is to choose properties that support both your real estate investment strategy and those that will enable you to fulfill your financial goals.

For the sake of example, let us say that your objective is to build a diverse portfolio that includes rental properties as well as fixer-uppers that you may rent out. You may want to start searching for rental homes with trustworthy, long-term tenants before starting any repair and flip efforts so that you may get them up and running.

How may risk be reduced while investing in real estate?

You may reduce risk by diversifying your real estate investment holdings. Your whole portfolio would be destroyed all at once, for instance, if all of your properties were located in a region that often experienced natural catastrophes or sharp market fluctuations. Look at various states and localities where investment makes sense.

What are the dangers of real estate investing?

Although real estate investment may be profitable, it is vital to be aware of the pitfalls. Bad sites, poor cash flows, large vacancies, and problematic renters are among the main hazards. The real estate market's unpredictability, latent structural issues, and a lack of liquidity are additional dangers to take into account.

Happy reading